CONTENTS

HOW TO USE THE CD ACCOMPANIMENT:

A MELODY CUE APPEARS ON THE RIGHT CHANNEL ONLY. IF YOUR CD PLAYER HAS A BALANCE ADJUSTMENT, YOU CAN ADJUST THE VOLUME OF THE MELODY BY TURNING DOWN THE RIGHT CHANNEL.

THE CD IS PLAYABLE ON ANY CD PLAYER, AND IS ALSO ENHANCED SO MAC AND PC USERS CAN ADJUST THE RECORDING TO ANY TEMPO WITHOUT CHANGING THE PITCH.

Series Artwork, Fox Trademarks and Logos
TM and © 2010 Twentieth Century Fox Film Corporation.
All Rights Reserved.

ISBN 978-1-4234-9503-1

HAL•LEONARD® CORPORATION
7777 W. BLUEMOUND RD. P.O. BOX 13819 MILWAUKEE, WI 53213

Visit Hal Leonard Online at
www.halleonard.com

◆ ALONE

ALTO SAX

Words and Music by BILLY STEINBERG
and TOM KELLY

② BUST YOUR WINDOWS

ALTO SAX

Words and Music by JAZMINE SULLIVAN,
SALAAM REMI and DEANDRE WAY

4

❸ AND I AM TELLING YOU I'M NOT GOING

from DREAMGIRLS

ALTO SAX

Music by HENRY KRIEGER
Lyric by TOM EYEN

mf

❹ DANCING WITH MYSELF

ALTO SAX

Words and Music by BILLY IDOL
and TONY JAMES

Copyright © 1981 Chrysalis Music Ltd. and Universal Music Publishing Ltd.
All Rights for Chrysalis Music Ltd. in the U.S. and Canada Administered by Chrysalis Music
All Rights for Universal Music Publishing Ltd. in the U.S. and Canada Controlled and Administered by Universal - PolyGram International Publishing, Inc.
All Rights Reserved Used by Permission

◆ IMAGINE

ALTO SAX

Words and Music by
JOHN LENNON

DEFYING GRAVITY

ALTO SAX

Words and Music by
STEPHEN SCHWARTZ

Allegro, as before

◆ DON'T STOP BELIEVIN'

ALTO SAX

Words and Music by STEVE PERRY,
NEAL SCHON and JONATHAN CAIN

◆8 KEEP HOLDING ON

from the Twentieth Century Fox Motion Picture ERAGON

ALTO SAX

Words and Music by AVRIL LAVIGNE
and LUKAS GOTTWALD

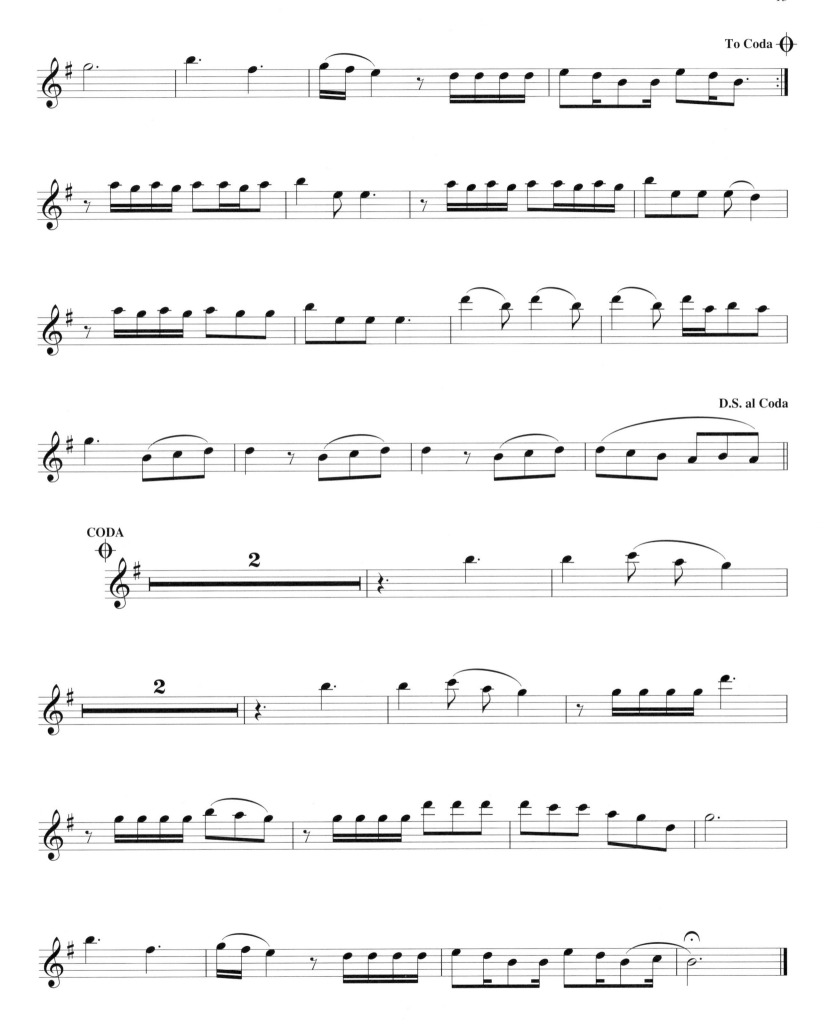

◆⑨ LEAN ON ME

ALTO SAX

Words and Music by
BILL WITHERS

◆10 MY LIFE WOULD SUCK WITHOUT YOU

ALTO SAX

Words and Music by LUKASZ GOTTWALD,
MAX MARTIN and CLAUDE KELLY

SWEET CAROLINE

ALTO SAX

Words and Music by
NEIL DIAMOND

◆12 NO AIR

ALTO SAX

Words and Music by JAMES FAUNTLEROY II,
STEVEN RUSSELL, HARVEY MASON, JR.,
DAMON THOMAS and ERIK GRIGGS

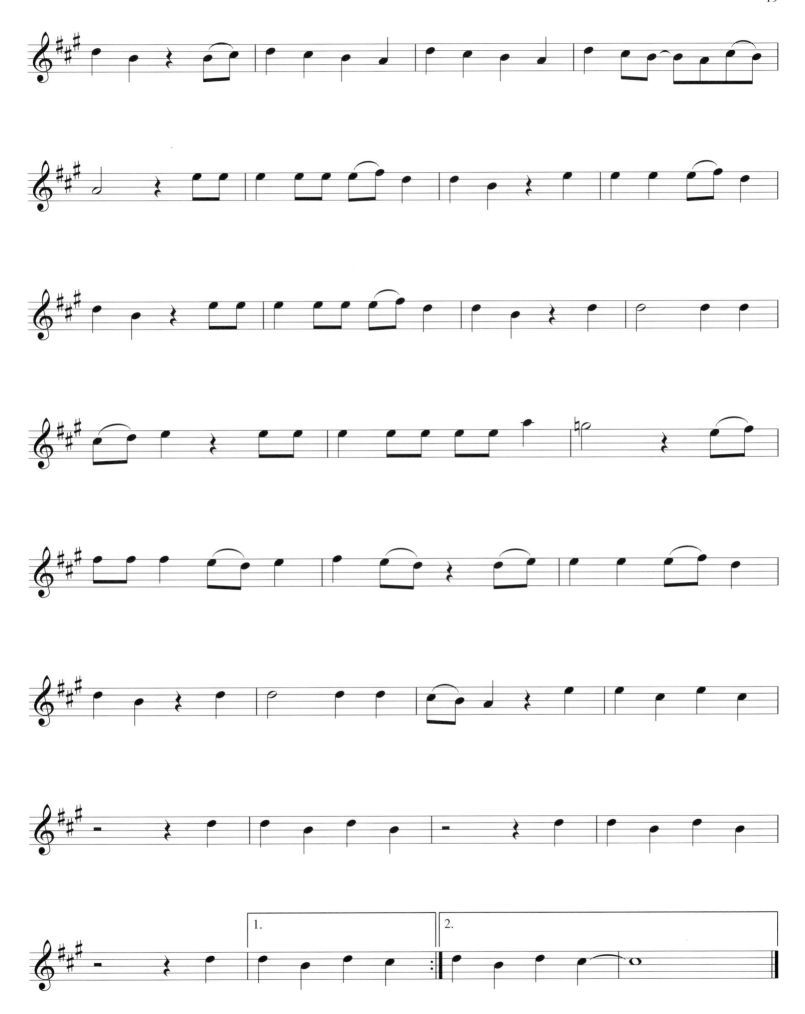

🔶 TAKE A BOW

ALTO SAX

Words and Music by SHAFFER SMITH,
TOR ERIK HERMANSEN and MIKKEL ERIKSEN

◆14 TAKING CHANCES

ALTO SAX

Words and Music by DAVE STEWART
and KARA DioGUARDI

TRUE COLORS

ALTO SAX

Words and Music by BILLY STEINBERG
and TOM KELLY